LETTERS, AND WHY THEY'RE ALL FOR YOU

letters, and why they're all for you

Written across the world.

First paperback edition July 4, 2016

ISBN 978-0-9946352-6-6

Original cover design and artwork by Jessica C. Barros

Single cat illustration by Haylee DeGoumois

LETTERS, AND WHY THEY'RE ALL FOR YOU

A POETRY SERIES

by

CHLOË FRAYNE

for Haylee
this book would not exist
if you didn't

for Amy and Evolette

and for my family,
whomever you may be -

if you read this, and I feel like yours,
write back.

All these romances,
all these letters
tucked inside envelopes
and cut upon pages.
All these stories
whispered to oblivion
and the unmistakable growl
of time.
All these beautiful words
existing for but one purpose –
one insistent
and remarkable truth:

you are loved.

I could write to you of her beauty
as I'm sure many others could,
but there is so much more.
My friend, I wish I could write you
her laugh.
I wish I could give you words and spaces
so remarkable to you
that you would hear her.
I wish I could point
to her galaxy eyes
and you would feel what it is
to be seen by her
because they are the only moments
when it matters
to be seen at all.

*Her soul is a flower
and I am drunk on the perfume, my friend.*

This story
and every one
I tell,
begins and ends
with you.

She said
"My hugs can fix anything"
and I prayed, I prayed they could
but the thing
the thing about it that saved me
was that
she
was trying to.

If I can do
one thing
in this world,
I hope I can give you
a collection of moments
when you felt okay.

I have always worried that
wishing for somebody
is selfish;
that if the universe heard
and granted that wish
we would be altering fate
on their behalf –
as though we
and not they
know what's best for them,
and it's us.
But what if we're wrong?
And what if they always knew
and that's why
we had to wish for them
in the first place?

'Haylee'

– God, on His best day.
(before wings were apostrophes)

Something quiet happens
in the time it takes
to want someone
and to reach for their hand,

and it is the fear
of the reach
and the bliss
of the take
which makes
the space between
paradise.

Every step you take
is a victory.

Make sure you're fighting
the right battles.

Perhaps
we inherited our obsession
with reflections
from the universe,
and the sky looks down
upon our cities of glass
and smiles.

Imagine that you're a puzzle.
The first few times you get broken up,
it's easy to put you together
it makes sense
the picture is still beautiful.
Then imagine that you stop breaking
where you're already broken.
Imagine that the pieces start breaking in
halves
quarters
sixteenths
and you lose some of the pieces
and there's water damage
and it doesn't even look like the picture anymore
and so everyone gets up
and leaves the table
because they don't know how
to put it back together.

That's depression.

Don't be afraid
to still believe
in fairytales
just because your
Happily Ever After
hasn't happened:

Cinderella was a slave
with dead parents
and bad shoes,
but her story wasn't over,
and neither is yours.

Three things will save you:
One: words
Two: love
Three: yourself.

Start with One and let them.

Let them save you.

To know that
at some point
every day
you
think of me

...

What the fuck else matters?

CHLOË FRAYNE

I fell
I fell like stars
like leaves in autumn
and snow from grey clouds
above your angel head.
I fell
and I was happy,
happy to land
in your outstretched hand.

You cannot possibly understand
until you're looking
down the barrel
of a life you don't want,
and you don't know
whether it will misfire
or you'll pull the trigger,

but you reach for it anyway.

It is strange that
even when our dreams
come true, they still feel
so unreal to us,
as though who we are
when we are asleep
and who we are
when we are awake
are different people,
and cannot comfortably
open their eyes
to the same life.

I wonder how many lives
would have been saved
if nobody was afraid
that it wasn't
their place
to save them.

I wonder how many lives
would have been saved
if nobody was afraid
that they wouldn't
be able
to save them.

I can't imagine
anything worse
than a world
without you in it.

She felt alone
because
the only arms
that held her
when she was broken
were the 42
of her typewriter.

She never swam
in the ocean
but she said
it made her feel
alive
because it connected her
to the moon
and reminded her
of a hopeful, distant shore
and the bravery
she would need
to come crashing down
upon it.

I used to start thinking
about you
in the morning
and now I start
at night
and you
are running
out
of

time.

I am not afraid
to die; for

every time
I fall in love,
I catch a glimpse
of Heaven.

She was
the only person
I had ever known
whose every kiss
was a wish.
She gave them carefully:
they were promises
and promises
are forever.

In this,
they did not understand
their betrayal:

Wishes
must never
be stolen.

In therapy he tells me that people will always
be around and talk to you more in the beginning
because they're getting to know you,
and once they feel like they do then you become
familiar, and slowly it turns into
more of a standard, check-in relationship.
I try to understand this because he says it like
it's normal. And I don't. So I try harder. But I can't.
You were probably alive for twenty or so years
before I met you.
Twenty years of you and versions of you
I'll never meet and people who loved and left you.
Days and nights and moments
when your heart was broken
and somebody was there, or they weren't.
There were near-deaths, nights when you wished
they were closer than 'near', victories,
quiet moments, violent enemies and
fucked up friends. You've had
weird accidents and funny days and moments when
your kindness has been overwhelming.
You've had anxious hours, hated flaws,
you've cried your pretty heart out.
You've been broken and mended
and there have been people who
brought you to both.

You've been happy.
You've had pets and friends and family
and they've all changed you
in thousands of ways because
you loved them and they loved you
and sometimes they didn't and I want to know that,
I want to know why and who and when and you –
I want to know you.
All of you, all of the You I've missed.
All of the You that you are now
and all of the You that you are becoming because
I don't want to miss that, miss you – this you,
the next you.

People are made of moments and each one is a story
and I want to know every single piece of you
and how they came together before we ever did.
I don't know how you're done so fast
but I'm not done with you.
I'm not.
And the thing is, your life is filled with moments
and I don't want to miss a single one
because I love you. I fucking love you.
I will go on loving you.
And I will never be done.

We followed Hope
to the ends
of the Earth,
and when we
finally caught him,

he told us the story
of how he fooled us all.

He dragged
on his cigarette
the way he dragged
his voice,
the way he dragged you:

like a fucking idiot.

How fragile a thing,
your love,
that it could be
destroyed
by one kiss.

Whenever I tried to describe it –
the way I've wanted you,
the way I've missed you –
the closest I ever came
to truth
was dehydration, starvation,
and as such
I felt at home in them.
Quite simply,
every cell
that collects within me
is screaming for you.

And when we say
goodbye
I will always wait
for you
to leave me first
because
every step I take
away from you
feels like a mistake.

You are a comet
passing by this world
and I am reaching for you,
trying not to reach for you,
but reaching for you.
You could never understand why,
but
I would burn
I would burn everything
if only it would end
with your fire.

I am sorry, sorrier
than I can ever tell you,
that anyone has ever
made you believe that
what you hate about yourself
should be hated,
but I must tell you this now,
and I hope you will believe me.
You are not beautiful
the way other people are beautiful.
You are beautiful
the way
the stars are beautiful,
and there will always be those
who are afraid
of the immensity, of the light.
But there will also be
astronomers,
stargazers,
and me.

I never understood
this world, these people
less
than when I saw
the way
they hurt you.

Some mighty and beautiful things
demand to be told.
Not just told,
told right.
The best of them, is this.
I love you like I love the moon:
tremendously, and completely,
and a little more every day.

The only thing
that stands between
Utopia
and Dystopia
is a little
Dysfunction
and no
U.

You know those "good at letting go" types?
I'm not one of them.
It'll take me three years to find a way
to be okay without you
and even then there's a good chance
you'll find me sitting on the bathroom floor
ten years later
crying 'cause you left.

There are glorious people
with the kind of eyes
others write stories about
and the kind of smiles
that end wars
and the kind of laughs
that bring you back to life,
and these people

they are waiting for you.

It's okay to feel sad
about stale toast on quiet mornings
and long car rides alone
and dirty bathwater at midnight
and crumpled "I-love-you"s at the end
and things that shouldn't be sad,
but are, because they're different now
without Them.

It's okay to be sad.
It's okay to sigh at the stars.
And it's okay to be the one
who cries at airports.

I am sorry
about your broken heart
but
have you ever seen a mosaic?

People who want luxury cars
and empty mansions
have always scared me.
What do you do with someone
who wants so much
when all you want is them?
And how do you survive
knowing you're not enough,
and they are?

Perhaps
some of us
have spent so long
with our heads
in the clouds
that we forget
we don't belong
with the stars.

She tells stranger souls
that she loves them –
every day, a different one:
trees and moths and beetles,
shafts of sunlight and clouds
and stars.
And when I asked her why,
she told me she had realised
that they might only
hear it once.

And we were all
just crashing
to an ending,
pretending
not to hear the sound.

I have always felt horribly that I have friends
not because I am loved but
because you are.
Because they love the you they find in me
they see me as an extension of somebody
they care about,
somebody they know,
and that somebody tells them I need it:
I need a warning label
I need to be treated carefully
like a bomb nobody wants to touch –
I am crazy;
all roads leading to me are paved
with eggshells
and obsessions
and the suffering Too Much,
she says.
And they believe
and I have pity friends
and you are not here
even when you are.

These words are nothing
but paper soldiers
lying on the battlefield
of Love
with your face
in their I's
and your sword
out their backs.

If somebody told me that I could have
everything I want in 2 years,
but not be able to see anyone I care about
because I'll be too busy, or
I can have it in 5, and still be with them,
I would choose them every goddamn time
and I would not have to think twice about it.
We're dying. All of us. We are.
And even if, by some miracle, someone you love
manages to live exactly as long as you do,
that wouldn't necessarily mean
that you'd still love each other,
and it wouldn't mean you'd still have them.
Because we're not only dying, we're changing.
Slowly, sometimes suddenly, we are doing both.
And maybe you'll still be You and they'll still be
Them
in 6 months, 2 years, a decade,
but maybe you won't.
Maybe your chance is right fucking now
and you're wasting it
thinking you'll take it next week, next year,
tomorrow, someday –

as though you're guaranteed that long,
or that time with Them.
But we aren't.

That person you love? You're losing them.

Do something about it.

When I have forgotten
how to live
the towns I lived in
the places I've been, and
the way back home;
When I have forgotten
how to remember
how to drive
the sound of your voice,
and the alphabet;
When I have forgotten
the patterns of the stars
the sound of an "I love you", and
how to breathe;
and even
When I have forgotten
my own name,
I will still remember
yours.

It's easy to forget
that the versions of people
we hold in our hands
and carry in our pockets
are just that:
versions.
It's easy to forget
that they exist somewhere,
real, full,
typing to you,
sending themselves,
missing you back.
It's easy to forget
that they smell
(and it's Them)
that their laugh has a sound
(and it's alive)
and there's their voice
(and it's safe)
and their presence
(and it's magic)
and the way they look at you
(and it's home).

I could never grow tired of love -
of writing about love,
about you;
of love songs
poetry
heartbreak
the way people look at each other
even when they're tired;
even when everyone else
is watching them;
even when to look
is to be brave
and bravery is something
they've long forgotten.
They look.
They breathe.
They remember.
And they're brave.

Forget the cynics,
that's beautiful.

People keep asking me
whether I'm afraid to go alone,
and I'm not.
No.
I'm afraid to stay alone.

She could not stop
running
and they did not
know why,
but she could not stop
hearing
the sound of doors closing
behind them
as they left,
and I held her hand
because
I could hear them, too.

Every day I've fought
to get through
without you
is a victory
I never wanted to win.

I was always afraid
of how alive you were.
It was incredible,
but I was afraid
you would ask me
to be alive with you,
and I wouldn't know how.

Or, worse,
that you wouldn't ask
at all.

It's important to recognise
that even a good person
can be bad for you.

Absence
has always hit me hard.
I feel the lack of you
far more than the presence.
And so I knew –
I knew leaving would suffocate me;
knew it would destroy me in a brand new way,
like only being farther from you
could do.
But in truth, I feel it already,
and I have for a long time.
Further or farther:
Without You here
or Without You there.
I might as well choose the one
that lets me tell you
I miss you.
I might as well
choose the one
that lets me pretend
that distance
is the reason why.

How beautiful it is
to see you here.
I **am** afraid
I have missed you
so much that **I**
am never
going to be able
to look away again,
to blink without grief,
to ever again allow
one of us to **leave**
this place where we're together,
where all I know is **you**.

There is a certain way
somebody looks at you
when they truly love you.
Wait for that.
Don't you dare settle
for anyone
who looks at you
like you're ordinary.

In everything I am,
in everything I do,
I want to be saying
I love you.
I want you to hear it
in the way I say goodbye,
the way I drive,
the way I look at you,
and the colour of my eyes.
I want it to whisper
through fingertips
and smile at you
from words on paper
and tell you always
of this remarkable truth.

In every breath
hides an 'I love you'
and they
all
belong
to you.

I live in a place
full of people
who don't care
about me.

And it's only okay
because
I'm one of them.

We dreamed
of beautiful things
we never held,
beautiful lives
we never had,
because we
always
felt too ugly
to belong to them.

Perhaps
we each possess
a heaven
that is not
our own.

I love you
in ways
and in spaces
that did not exist
before you
and cannot exist
when you are gone.
I love you
in a sadness
that is alive
when you are not
and dead
while you are living.

When we loved,
we called them
kings and queens,
and tried to forget
that they called us
peasants.

The faster we ran
the sicker we got
and they shouted
from the sidelines,
screaming for us to stop;
but we could not hear,
we did not listen,
for to us they were ghosts
taking bets on who survives,
and so we cried
as we ran
for our lives.

I miss you
and I look for you
everywhere I go
but we
are thousands of miles
apart,
and these stars
are the only ones here
who know your name.

I dreamed of places
where now I've been,
and you're still
the best thing
I've ever seen;
and in the end,
when I came home,
you're still
the best thing
I've ever known.

I want nothing more
than to hear you say
I hate you.
And I want nothing more
than to know
that you don't mean it.

How often
Love
shoulders
the blame
for the
troubles
of Doubt.

And we are all
just fighting
to survive a world
where
I miss you
doesn't mean
I'm coming back,
and
I love you
doesn't mean
I'll stay.

Some people are only
in our lives
long enough to show us
what it is
to be happy,

so we know
what to chase
when they are gone.

Her disease, she said, had a hunger.
It fed on hope
and the bones in her mind
and the light of her soul.

First it devoured her body,
then it devoured her life,
then it devoured her desire for either.

She was uncomfortable in her body
and she was uncomfortable in the hiding
and so she tore
tore her flesh down to bone
to escape it all

and she was free
and she was okay
and we did not mourn her.

Imagine how much is lost
in the silence between people.
Days and months and broken eternities
we promised yet never gave.
I see it in their faces
as they walk down the street
and it's silence,
always silence
screaming back,
and I wonder why on Earth
we are such mysteries to one another
even though I am listening for you -
following a sound
you have yet to make
with the unfaltering belief
in love,
only love.

I will find a way
to love you
in moments
and not years.

Something within me
is screaming and singing
at the same time
and it cries
because it knows you hear it.
It knows you are listening
and loving us
for the music
and the chaos
and the beauty of the weeping
and, God,
does it smile
for you.

Sometimes when I'm with someone
all I can concentrate on is their breathing.
I can feel them breathing and I just sit there
listening to it
and feeling it
and thinking about how fucking beautiful it is.

The best kind of people
carry Good and Bad in extremes,
and what matters
is that they are not suffocated
by either side.
They drown in both
and they breathe
because they fucking have to.
They survive because it would be
an unforgivable injustice of the universe
to stop them.
They are people of insanity and
all the goddamn miraculous courage in the world
and we love their brokenness
for all that it is
and all that it never will be
because that, my friend,
is how to love somebody.
That is how we look
upon the cruel face of Sadness
and shout so loudly that it shrinks away.
That is how we save them.
That is how they save us.
I know
because that is how she saved me.

There is a magic in you
that cannot be
stripped away
by this world, these people;
but I am sorry to say,
some of them will try.

And if you are afraid,
please know

Even if being special
is not enough,

you are.

I fall in love all the time.
I think there are a lot of ways to be in love,
you know?
I think hearts are capable of so much more.
I am in love with places
and the clouds above them
and the things that exist quietly behind.
I am in love with mystery and magic,
the sparkling of wonder
and the golden of imagining.
I am in love with words and stories
and the voices that treasure them.
I am in love with the battled and beaten
and glorious age;
with the mightiness of the natural world
and the gentles it carries.
I am in love with souls and with light
and the way that they are the same thing.
I am in love with the moon and the world,
the stars and the spaces between them.
I fall in love with brokenness
and the songs that sing to it
and the people who are drowning
but still find ways to breathe.

I am in love with kinks in eyebrows
and galaxy eyes
and smiles even when they're sad.
I am in love with the way the world looks at you
and with the way you look back;
the sound of people laughing
and how goddamn beautiful they are when they cry.
I am in love with the punctured souls
and the universe they spin inside
and nothing,
nothing is ugly.

We cast our fear
upon the clouds
and watched our faith
fall in rain
and we searched for something
that would turn
our white knights
into saviours
and our nightmares
into happy endings
beside them.

They said
"This will save you"
and

I traded in
the bones of my body
for the bones
of my soul
but

I was not saved
until you said
"I love you."

I carry them
in my mind,
like ghosts
I could not
leave behind

and

there is a darkness
so divine,
that holds us close
from time to time.

The loud became
silent
the silent became
beautiful
the beautiful became
her.

If life
is nothing but a garden,
then every day
amongst the trees
has taught me that
our most beautiful flowers
are terrified
of the sun.

They lost their minds
by no real loss
from no mistake
but because
they could not
survive them.

I said to her
"You know how
I'm looking for my family?
I think you're part of it."

And she told me
we had known that
since we were kids –
as simply as though
saying it
hadn't changed a thing
because it had always
been true.

And that,
above all else,
is how I knew
we were right.

There was no
alone
as long as
there was
her.
And in the end
the best way
to fight for her
was to find
a way
to stay.

Days
like falling stars
that are not
wishes
but the death
of something
beautiful.

It seems to be
that people are bored
with the way I love them
long before I am finished
being fascinated
with the way
they walked through the door.

Have you ever loved
a human so beautiful that
you cannot see
lonely colours
every time your
eyes close?

Return me now
to a time
when we could fall asleep
without
falling apart.

Because
I don't know how
to look at you
like I'm not in love with you.
And
you don't know how
to look at me
like that's okay.

There is a lake
filled with more salt than water
where I buried a piece of paper
beneath grains of time
bathed in pink;
where I prayed
where I lived
where I made a wish for you,
and you alone;
where I asked for you
the kind of joy
people write stories about
for a hundred years;
where I loved you
without secret
without quiet
without end.

I could live
my entire life
caught
in the moments
of people's faces
lighting up
when they see mine.

I could live
my whole life
in those moments
and never get tired
of your face.

I hate when people try to tell you
how it'll get easier to miss somebody.
It won't.
It'll get subconscious.
You won't even realise how sad you are.
You won't consciously think about why
but you'll feel it.
And then your song will come on the radio
and it'll be like they're leaving you
all over again.
Only this time,
everyone expects you to be okay.

There is a silence
that is not divine
is not peaceful
and is not absolute,
and in the distant, shivering whispers,
I can still hear you.

There are flowers
in your soul
and I want to know
who planted them.

I hope it was you.

The sky is littered with little planes
filled with little people
and none of them are you.
The ground is filled with litter and broken bodies
and none of them are you.
The world is filled with perfectly decent people
living perfectly ordinary lives
with perfectly ordinary souls,
and none of them
are you.

They spent so many years treating me
like a pathetic creature needing and wanting them
more than they thought I should,
and somewhere along the way
I stopped telling people
because it felt like this shameful, selfish little secret.
And I convinced myself that it should be
because if they wanted me
as much as I wanted them
then I wouldn't need to ask;
I wouldn't be the only one.
All of a sudden
it felt like I was asking for this huge favour:
be around, be around more.

I need you.
I want you.
I am not afraid.

You rise and you are beautiful
but you are not beautiful for them –
you are beautiful because it is your nature;
it is your sunrise, your sunset
your breath upon the dust of the earth
and the sighs of the morning
and the unimaginable brokenness of time
and the souls who desperately cling to it.

You are here
and you love me
and for the first time,
everything is going to be okay.

She sat
upon the moon
and set her sights
upon our hope.
Her sighs
crashed in waves
and her tears
were the stars;
as endless
and beautiful
and heartbroken
as the stars.

People pull out their label makers
and stick the word Obsessive over me
like I should be offended
and in truth I used to be
but no more.
I am obsessive and so I will notice you
all of you
not just the parts that are easy to notice.
I will remember you
not just the evidence of you but
remember your stories and the things you love;
not just the things you say you love
not just the things I want you to love.
I will think about you
and you
and everything about you
and I will fall in love with that
and this
and everything that makes you and me
we.
I guess what I'm trying to say is
I will be gloriously fascinated
by you

and the unearthly goodness
of loving you,
of being loved by you.
I am obsessive and so I will write about you
I will write about it
I will write about us.
And someday,
perhaps you will understand
and the word will become beautiful
to you, too.

We make fun of them for excited voices
And the things that cause it
And our slow-gotten jokes.
We make fun of them for how they dress
And how they talk
And the things they love
And the way they love them.
We make fun of them for their number on a scale
And their number on a test sheet
And their number in our line.
We make fun of them for the way they dance
And the way they laugh
And the way they breathe.
We make fun of them for their sadness
And their pain
And their inability to hide either.
We make fun of them for humanness.
Then we make fun of them for being afraid.
Then we make fun of them for killing themselves.

We comforted ourselves
with delusions
and I
fucking hated us
for it.

Here's the thing, my friend:
We are losing them.
We are losing them to the silence
and then telling them we still love them
and I swear to you,
they don't buy it.
There is something missing in us
that leaves them waiting
and we do not make it stop;

we never make it stop.

I ran away
to save myself
and took only
what I needed.

I packed a suitcase
of our good days
and left
everything else
on the highway.

Sometimes you lose people
not because you're not good enough
but because
you're so convinced
that you're not.

Sometimes I wish I could go back in time
and live my life in the moments
when I had you.

And then I realise
I do the same thing
every day
in my head.

I once had a conversation with a man
who did not understand my lack of religion.
He asked "Then what do you believe in?"
I said "I believe in a lot of things,
I'm just not sure God is one of them.
I believe in people, and magic and words
and love."
He did not understand and so he told me
that when he wakes in the morning
he prays to God
and thanks Him for his life.
He asked me what I pray for when I pray,
and at the time I said I don't.
But then I realised
I had prayed eight times since I came to Africa
and I always prayed for you.

They wonder
if lonely falling trees make sounds
but they do –
they all do:
they are screaming
and we wonder why
as we walk away
through selfish fires
lit
by matches we threw.

She only liked herself in photographs
where she was looking at someone else,
because she looks at people
like she's in love with them,
and she says
she can't get enough of the girl
who can't get enough of you.

We are fucking magic,
my loves;

we will not be crushed
by the mountains,

we will not be drowned
by the sea.

They said
"welcome home"
and I knew I was supposed to say
I was glad to be back.

But I couldn't.

There were shouts –
a thief in the night –
people were gathered to watch
red, red light
of fire against dark sky,
and the fire was a man
and we watched him burn

but the only thief I met
was his scream
which stole
every peaceful sleep
I've never had since.

I am in love with the way
people look at one another.

People have a habit
of getting stuck in my head
like songs:
they play on repeat for days,
and I cannot stop seeing
the way you smiled
when you looked at me.

She admitted she kept me
like a caged bird
because she was afraid
to be alone,
and she knew
I would take all her excuses
with me
if I left.

It's funny
how much we can admit
with silence.

She told me
"In the end, everything
comes down to money."
And I said
"I can't believe you're this old
and you still don't understand
that life is about love."

How strange to think
you can live lifetimes
in someone's head
from days
by their side.

I have imagined one hundred
different scenarios
in which we never met
and I suppose there are probably
one hundred different dimensions
where that has happened
but if I know anything
in this one, it's that
every single version of me
is looking for you.

You know that look
in someone's eyes
when they see you?

Don't fuck that up.

The worst part of waiting for
someone to come back to you
is knowing even if they did,
they changed everything
when they left,
and that's not coming back with them.

The thing is,
we lose people
in one hundred
small ways
before we ever
lose them
in a big one

and the problem
with me is,
I can't stop noticing.

People will find all kinds of ways
to control you, and I am sorry to say,
fear is the most common technique,
and they won't care that no matter
how deep you dig,
you can't pull it back out.
I know that's how he did it
and I know I never could.
I guess even then phonebooks were
symbolic,
because he would slam one on the table
and dare us to call someone to stop him.

And I guess it worked
because we never did.

I will never understand
why
thankfulness for your life
requires the taking
of someone else's.

How beautiful it is,
the way people collide.
It is all I see,
everywhere I go.
People light up like stars
when they look at someone they love,
and it is heartbreaking
to wonder how long they waited –
but isn't it beautiful?
We are a universe of
Christmas lights,
blinking all the time.

I carry you with me
everywhere I go, and
I look for you in stars
you have never seen,

but now everywhere I go
is a place where you
have been.

I looked at these people
who pretended to want me
and I dared them
to be in my life
more than my head...

I guess they finally picked Truth.

I think sometimes part of the allure
of "run away with me"
is not the leaving
so much as the idea that
someone would leave with you
and be okay
because you're all they need.

And I think sometimes
when we ask,
that is our real question.

I don't know how to talk to
or look at people
like I'm not in love with them.
For the longest time,
I let people say there was something bad
or wrong about that,
and I let it affect me;
I let it change what I said,
how much I said
who I said it to –
but no more. No.
I will look at you like you are the stars
and I will speak to you
as though my words
are the only ones to save you
because God knows,
they could be.

She was better than anyone
and I didn't know how
to let her go

and that terrified me
until the day I realised
I don't have to let her go.

I have to be worthy
of holding on.

She was fleeting foxes
through ancient forests
glowing in dappled sunlight
that greeted her
through the fingers
of beautiful giants
beneath cloudless skies,
and she was happy there,
and she was everything good
in this goddamn world.

And you burnt her forest to the ground
and laughed in the ashes
as we lost her
we all lost her
and we lost ourselves
in the process –
but, God,
we deserved to.

We see all these people
ruining their lives
because they think they are obliged
to spend time with people
who ruin them,
and we pity them for this –
but why?
If we turn our heads
we see seas of people
waiting to love them
and we shout over the roar;
we tell them to look,
but they look at us
and they look away
and they never know.

And so we pity them.
We just go on pitying them.

He traced the lines
between my bullet holes
as he swore on my life
we were not at war.

There is something to be said
about tragedy –
some reckless abandon that follows,
some beauty in rebirth,
in the moments between a woman crying
and a child taking her hand;
some danger
in the ones who notice.

For never doubt
that beauty can destroy us
just as swiftly
as chaos.

You know what?
Let someone in.
Don't you dare sit there and say it's hard for you,
and you're scared and you don't think
they'll love you.
It's hard for everyone. Everyone is scared.*
And if they don't love you after
then they never fucking did.
Go split yourself open and pour out everything
you never say to anyone, and when you're empty
and raw and somehow feel
both broken and connected,
dig a bit deeper and let them in a little further,
and then open your pretty eyes and notice that
they're still standing right in front of you.
Because it wasn't anything to be ashamed of.
It never was.
And they still think you're beautiful.

(*Everyone is scared.)

The world burned
and the fabric of the universe
opened, and let it fall through;
birds flew by flaming trees
with nowhere left to land
and nowhere safe to hide
and none of it mattered
as much as the fact that
you were the one
meant to save it.

There are 6 days
23 hours
59 minutes
and an eternity
between
how long it takes me
to miss you, and
how long it takes you
to miss me back.

Steel feet
that crushed helicopters
and spirits
and little girls' ribs,

and screams
that echoed
in heads
that weren't listening.

It's easy to be shiny
and to paint your life with glitter
when everyone is looking
and nobody wants to see,
but some people go home
and wash their faces
and destroy the world
with everything underneath.

I still don't know whether
the problem is that I thought
my family would feel more for me
than this, or the problem is that
this
is not them.

How difficult it is
to be
the kind of person
to come alive
when someone you love
looks at you,
and still remember
you exist
when they don't.

Every night
I fall asleep terrified,
feeling like
something is missing
and I'm forgetting
something important

and I just keep praying
it's not you.

But does there exist
a greater heartbreak
than the knowledge
that everything wilts
in the winter
of existence?

And the day will come
when we must
dry our tears
to shed our masks,
and unveil
the hideous wonder beneath.

Sometimes I wonder
how I will manage
to get through
the rest of my life
without you,

and then I think,
"The same way
I have been
all this time:

barely."

All it takes is one person.
One person to make everything wonderful.
One person to colour your world with infectious
beauty.
One person to change your life.
One person to change you.
And the discovery of such a person –
that you found them
or they found you
or the world found you both –
reawakens the fire that
has long been extinguished,
and is extraordinary indeed.

She had grown so detached and lost
from herself
that the skeletal remains
of her former person
no longer bore any resemblance
to the creature
she had become.

There are a lot of ways to lose somebody.
You can lose them when Death
opens his hungry mouth
and swallows them whole.
You can lose them when the universe
tears you apart.
You can also lose them because it only
tore one of you.
But there are other, less glorious ways
to lose somebody.
You can lose them because they wanted to be lost.
Sometimes they do not know they have already
started to leave.
Sometimes, they have begun a game
of hide-and-seek
and forgotten to tell you that
they want you to find them.
Sometimes the losing happens
because you never figure it out.
And sometimes the losing happens
because they never wanted you to.

I lost you quietly.
(Quietly for you.)

How deeply human it is
to know that
there are billions
of beautiful sights
in this world,
and none
call to our eyes
so intimately
and persistently
as faces.

If you ever desire
to question your beliefs,

fall in love

then as yourself
if they exist
by something
so unspectacular
as coincidence.

Your heart
deserves someone
who won't break it
on purpose.

Sadness
is capturing and limited
and can be good.
Unhappiness
lingers, and twists beneath
and cuts away at anything that rises above
okay.

We'll be friends or you'll be my family
and I will look at you like I'm in love with you
because that is the only way I know how.
In a way, in my way, I will be.
You'll either understand that or you won't
and it'll either be beautiful to you or it won't
and either way that's okay because sometimes
loving someone means doing what's best for them
no matter what it means for you.
There will always be people who will sit there
and say that the way I love you
is weird and obsessive and too much
and that's okay, too –
not because it won't hurt me
but because they're wrong
and the right people will know that.
The way I love you will be innocent and bold
and push us so far outside what we're used to
and I will be in love with that feeling.
There are so many ways to love,
to be in love,
and I do not for one second believe
that one is bigger or truer than another.
Your greatest loves will be yours.

They might be your pets or your children
or your husband or wife
or they might be your friends
or your home
or the feeling you get
when you listen to that song on that day, and
it will be beautiful no matter where it comes from
because it will be yours.
I will be yours and you will be mine
and there will be people who won't understand that.
But I will not build my life
on the expectations of the so-called norm.

And you know what?
That's okay.

The crazy thing is that no matter how much
it fundamentally disturbs us,
no matter how disgusted and hurt we are
with that part of you,
we are still expected to act as though it's okay.
We see murderers and genocide
and people we love being indifferent to both
and we are expected to forgive you for that.
No –
we are expected to believe there is
nothing to forgive.
And we try
because we love you -
of course we try.
But sometimes I watch you and I think
"That was a someone.
That was a someone and you took
their Someone away."

The more time
I spend with you
the more certain I am
that I'm not
good enough,
and the closer
I think you get
to realising.

I love movies and television shows,
but they're goddamn liars, you know?
They have these people who start out shit
and do shitty, sad, stupid things
and then they learn and become
golden souls full of change and new beginnings.
But change is not such a sure thing,
and too many people
just go on
being shit.

I want you to be with people who
are happy
and alive
and will never limit you,
and I'm just not one of them.
The quiet asphyxiation of your soul
will surprise you
when you realise I'm the one doing it.
And I'm sorry. I'm so sorry.
If I could be good for anyone,
I swear to God it would be you.

For people like me, I think when you love anyone
this much, they break your heart.
And that's okay.
Sometimes being broken is the best way
to love somebody.
You feel whole when you're with them.
You understand their brokenness in a way
unbroken people never could.
Maybe you're not whole and they're not whole
because you were always meant to be together,
and maybe being broken by them
will finally put you together
in a way that you need,
in a way that leaves you
a little less fractured.

One day he said,
"So is any one person's happiness
more important than another?"

I looked at him for a long while
and said,
"If one of those people is me
and another is her,
then yes."

Forgive yourself
for the person you were
in high school.

I had a conversation with a man once
where he told me that I love people like
I have blinkers on – the kind men put on horses.
And he said to me,
that it's a good thing when it focuses you on a career
but not on people.
I can't quite seem to not be bothered
by the idea that careers are more important
than people.

It continues to be hard to believe,
how wrong he was.
Because I see everything, my friend.
I see it all.
I just want you more.

This year
you have
24
extra hours.
Maybe
you can
use them
to
finally learn
how
not
to waste them.

Beer is one of those drinks
that has fanatics.
They look at you incredulously
when you say "No, thank you"
and they laugh like you're weird
so you feel like you have to explain yourself.

Truth is, judgmental stranger,
if it's been thrown at you enough times,
nothing tastes good anymore.

Isn't it funny how even monsters
can wake up in the morning
and put their Normal People clothes on
and trick real normal people into believing
they're Good, just by being Nice,
and normal people have never had
to question the difference
so they have no fucking idea
and they just go about their lives
swearing to God
these are people.

I was speaking to a woman
who was supposed to love me
but doesn't,
and telling her the ways
her indifference had hurt me,
and after two decades of weakness
and one final chance to be Something,
all she had to say to me was
"Well, I don't know what to do about it."

So I looked her dead in the eyes
and said
"Be better to me."

One day
as we sat on the porch of a house
in Bukibokolo,
I was listening to the radio with a man
and he began to question me about
which religion I belonged to.
When I said I wasn't religious,
he said "Oh,"
and after a few moments
he looked at me very seriously
and said
"You need to be saved."

I've seen dozens of horror movies
and I'll tell you, none of them unnerved me and
none of them were creepier
than when I was standing on a road
of a remote Ugandan village
and a little girl pointed her machete at me
and smiled.

You will leave your home
thinking you're going to miss everyone,
and you just won't.
Suddenly it will be obvious to you
how many people you're okay without.

There's a whole world out there
filled with people who are gonna love you,
so why is yours filled with people
who don't?

If you don't feel it curling in your soul
when you say 'I love you',
stop saying it.

I want people
who want me
so much that
I don't have
reason
to doubt them.

I want people
who prove
that Always
is just
as important
as Forever.

Miscommunication
is the thief of certainty of the humans you love.
You get this doubt in your head that
they do the things they do and
say the things they say because
they don't feel the way you do,
but you don't tell them it's there
and they don't tell you that you're wrong
and somewhere inside that convinces you
that you're not.
But what if you told them?
What if they never made you ask?
How terrifying it is that every person we love
has these big questions and thoughts and doubts
and we will never know
because we are all so afraid.
I'm sorry it's hard for you to let people in
because I know there's a Why.
But I am also sorry for doubt,
and the things it does to people.

So learn.

I just want to love you
like that's the only thing in this world
I was made for.

Because it is.

When I look into her eyes
I see pieces of the stars,
and I cannot help
but wonder
who owned the sky
that stole the rest.

There are too many souls walking this earth
with dead eyes
and heavy shoulders
and this fear in their bellies
that love
is not enough.
Then comes the day when they panic
because they realise they're hopeless.
So they have their children
and they stare into their eyes
and greedily feed their souls
with the forgotten spark they find inside
and for a moment
they are okay.

But all children grow up.

"It's just the way people are."
No.
Be better than that.
Accepting bad things as normal
destroys your will to change them.
Don't sit there and think it's okay
because everyone else does it.
No they don't. Not everyone.
Don't be one of them.
Make a decision to be a better person
and then go and fucking be one.

Here's the fucking thing, okay:
People will destroy you.
It'll suck.
It'll hurt.
But it might be the best thing for you.
Empty out the shit about you that you hate
and start to love people in the way
where you carry a part of them in your soul.
Fill yourself back up with them
and whenever you hate yourself
so much that you can't imagine anyone
wanting to know you,
remember that you're not just you,
you're a collection of Them –
of people you respect and admire
and think are wonderful;
of people you already love.
Use that to learn to feel the same way
about the rest of you.
There are so many relationships that begin and
bloom
and end with words you hold in your hand.
But when your phone dies, you'll forget.
You'll forget so much.

One day that person won't be around or
those versions of you and you together will be over,
and one day that phone will be gone
and you will never
have another new text or message or voicemail
or phone call
from someone you love
and you will not remember
most of the ones you did have.
The only evidence you will have of you together
will be in your head, and your head will fail you.

Someday one of us won't be here.
And if I'm ever without you,
I don't want to forget when I wasn't.
I want all of the evidence of us there is
and I want it to remind me that
I used to be an Us,
and there used to be a time
when I held hands
instead of old words.

I get that people change and everything changes
but I know so many people who have
absolutely no idea why things are so different
between them and someone else,
and to me, that is tragic.
Not the thing itself, but that
nobody asks and nobody tells
and everybody is confused and hurt and alone
and the people who swore they would never leave
have left; one day their Nevers
just became your brand new reality
and they still didn't tell you why,
and you still didn't ask.
You deserve better and they deserve better
and nobody stands up to be Better.
Everyone has their reasons and I get it, I do,
but not knowing what they are
leaves people in pretty terrible places.
You leave them in pretty terrible places.

Change is okay.
But if it affects someone else in a big way,
you should talk to them about it.

They're in this with you.
At least, they used to be.

One of the greatest mistakes people make
is to plan for Someday like it's a day of the week.
Today is someday. Tomorrow is someday.
Twenty years from now is someday.
We are losing our dreams and our people
simply because
we are giving each other nothing but promises
that don't demand to be kept.
Every person you love is waiting
for their goddamn Someday
and there is someone who desperately wants
their Someday with you
and it will never fucking happen
because we put a little hope on the horizon
and that's exactly where it stays.

I go outside and I am sure
this world is alive as a whole:
a being, an entity, Something –
with a capital S.
But I stand there, listening
to it breathing, and
I feel like I'm waiting
to hear a heartbeat.
It is surely far away,
deep down and hidden,
as it must be
to survive mankind –
but I listen for it still,
everywhere I go.

And, damn, when I'm with you,
if I don't have my fingers
on the pulse.

And we were
nothing
but a crowd
of stick people,
holding hands
and praying
for the strength
and serenity
to be
human beings.

They have this ridiculous idea that you should only
share the shiny parts of your life –
but let me tell you, they are so goddamn wrong.
There are billions of people in this world
and I promise you
that every single one of them has felt alone.
But they're not and they don't have to be
and neither do you.
People keep themselves like secrets.
Don't you dare fucking tell them to do that.
The way you feel is a secret,
your brokenness is a secret,
your failures are secrets,
your insecurities are secrets,
and you spend all your time
trying to think of "good" things to say
because they teach you to be afraid of the rest.
That's not okay. Those parts of yourself,
they will connect you to people
who understand, and those people will love you
in ways the rest of them won't
because you will be the reason
they don't feel alone anymore.

You will be the Someone
who trusted them with yourself,
who finally wanted those parts of them in return.

Nobody will ever know you
if you only give them the easy things.
You will feel alone until you stop fucking doing that.
Let them know you.
Tell someone.
Tell everyone.
Say something.
Speak.

Let
Someone
In.

And God, don't be alone.

Perhaps
it is more than science
that keeps the Earth and its moon
together.
Perhaps
it, too, is love
and they are spinning
always
in magnetic affections.

In my life I have trusted just one man
and we loved one another
but it was not enough.
And now I'm thinking about how
it only took a moment for him to give up
and a year
to forget to love me back.
And he sends me our song
and tells me it's too late,
that he didn't fight for me
because he didn't want to argue
and I cry myself to sleep thinking
"Who is this boy
and what has he done
with the man who loved me."

I'm here with nothing but
11:11 wishes
arcade tickets
ringpull keychains
bottle caps
movie stubs
one white rabbit
and
a headful of you
and they peek at me from corners of my room
and ask me what has happened
and I don't have an answer
because you never gave me one
and I can't understand how I can feel so guilty
for not being able to answer them
and you can not feel guilty at all
for leaving us asking.

(Suppose I'm just good at letting go.)

She whispers "I love you"
through the phone, and
I wonder about all of the 'I love you's
she will whisper in her life
and will it be a long one
will it be happy?
All of the souls she will whisper to,
I wonder will they deserve it?
Will they hold her hand
and fight beside her
and tell her everything will be okay
even when it won't?
Will they make sure it will be?
Will they say they love her back?
I want nothing more for her than
the kind of people who will;
and who won't forget.
Until them
after them
I will hold her hand

and I won't forget,
I won't forget.

How beautiful
and complicated it is
to find a home
in a person –
to feel complete and safe
beside them,
yet homesick
all the moments you're not;
how terrifying
to never be sure
when it will end.

How simple it must be, then,
to call a house your home –
how easy to return yourself
to something
that cannot leave you.

The best moments
of my life
are spent
standing still
on a crowded street;
hundreds of faces
coming toward me,

and then I see yours.

If you are reading this
before we have met
before we know what we're going to know
before we save each other,
then please know, little dove,
I have been searching for you
in faces that are not your own
in towns you have never seen
in hearts that have not known yours.
I have waited for this very moment
for this day for this hour, for this you
and this me.
I have wanted you and dreamed of you
and asked the moon to take care of you
(I hope you have been okay)
and you are finally here
this is it
and *I am finally home*.
If you are reading this
and you know why –
thank you.
You have already saved me.

I hope I saved you, too.

For as long as I can remember,
I have been afraid.
I have lived all my life
in a house of violence,
and it has taught me
fundamentally
instinctively
to be afraid.
I would open my eyes
and the world would exhaust me
fight or flight fight or flight.
The first time I felt safe
was the day I found you –
it was just so:
the safest place I'd ever found
was in the space around you.
My house was irrevocably nothing,
and You were home.

Perhaps
we are all searching
for someone
to teach us
that we
are not a burden.

My imagination
will carry me through
a thousand lifetimes
I could have lived with you.

"I trust you. I trust us.
I don't want to be careful.
I may be insecure as fuck
and I may not be sure
about a lot of things,
but I'm sure about you."

If you were looking
for someone
to be unaffected
by you,

you came
to the wrong person.

She was the kind of person
who made you believe with every breath
that the world was perfect –
undeniably so –
with the tremendous knowledge
that she exists in it.

She is a universe
of romance and beautiful chaos
spinning madly
in the dust
of possibility.
Her soul is a galaxy
and I swear to you
the constellations of her stars
will map your way home.

Write back.

CHLOË FRAYNE
P.O. BOX 788
WILLUNGA
SOUTH AUSTRALIA
AUSTRALIA
5172

LETTERS, AND WHY THEY'RE ALL FOR YOU

(if you have found me,
            thank you.)

Made in the USA
Lexington, KY
10 July 2019